**ANCHOR BOOKS**

CHASING RAINBOWS

Edited by

Sarah Andrew

First published in Great Britain in 2002 by
ANCHOR BOOKS
Remus House,
Coltsfoot Drive,
Peterborough, PE2 9JX
Telephone (01733) 898102

HB ISBN 1 84418 000 X
SB ISBN 1 84418 001 8

FOREWORD

Anchor Books is a small press, established in 1992, with the aim of promoting readable poetry to as wide an audience as possible.

We hope to establish an outlet for writers of poetry who may have struggled to see their work in print.

The poems presented here have been selected from many entries. Editing proved to be a difficult task and as the Editor, the final selection was mine.

I trust this selection will delight and please the authors and all those who enjoy reading poetry.

Sarah Andrew
Editor

CONTENTS

SELECTIVE MEMORY LOSS

It seems now you are older Mum
You selectively forget
The times that you had played the fool
And things that you regret.

'There was never any violence
And our elders were respected,
We never, ever broke the law
And Satan was rejected.'

I don't believe a word of it!
Perfect worlds just don't exist
Then and now are all the same
Some'll always speak with fists.

Dad's much more realistic
He says he knows that he did wrong
But then quickly looking awkward
Changes the subject before long.

I'm sorry to have to say it
But you've often been at fault
So admit it like the rest of us
Like you know you ought.

Sarah Sadler (14)

IMPOSSIBLE TO REACH

Cold and distant
She stares defiantly at me
How I wish that
She would open up
So I could see
Her emotions; what does she feel?

You can tell she is different
She seems so unreal
Face soft and rounded
Yet long lashes hide steel eyes
That look so wounded.

Her eyes tell a story
Within that look of lead -
So wrapped in her tragic past
She no longer cares what anyone's said.

I look deep into the face of that girl
I see something she wishes I hadn't seen
She wants to cover it from the world
But I listen to things that from within
Her head I heard.

I see the look of desperation in her face
Distorted beyond recognition
I am so near to her
Yet impossibly far away.
No one can reach her.
A tear trickles down my face.
And I push the mirror away.

Charlotte E Webb

THE SNOW AND FROST

The snow fell softly down toward the ground,
It almost looked like two hundred little white fairies
                                    dancing in the breeze.
The moon's beam was a shimmering silver as the stars
                              twinkled like specks of fairy dust.
The frost turned the pond into a plate of ice
Which looked like silver and white glitter had been sprinkled over it.
It was silent and magic as the snow fell quietly and swiftly.
Not a sound could be heard except a very thin breeze that
                              was rustling the trees.
The jingle of bells coming from the sky sounded like a fairy
                              singing a lullaby.
It was a bitterly cold night, almost as if Jack Frost had
                              done his work extra long.
The breeze gave a silent 'hush' and stopped.
Everything fell asleep . . .

Claire Cinnamon (8)

MY GRANDAD'S MYSTERIOUS FAIRY

My grandad says there's a fairy
That's only two inches tall,
She lives in the bottom of his garden
Just by the old brick wall.

He says he goes to visit her
Each and every day,
He takes her food, he takes her drinks,
He takes her toys to play.

She feeds on plants and other shrubs,
With the occasional glass of red wine,
The odd plate full of extra-large grubs.
This fairy knows how to dine!

So if strange things occur in your garden
Or things go bump in the night,
It could be Grandad's fairy
Ready to give you a fright!

I never really believe my grandad
When he speaks of this mysterious fairy,
But if she really does exist,
My advice is to be weary!

Tanya Jade Johnson (11)

FOOD, FOOD, FOOD

Apples, pears, peaches and plums,
Strawberry tart and current buns,
These are the things I like to eat,
Because they all taste very sweet!

Cabbage, sprouts, peas and swede,
These are things I do not need,
But they are placed upon my plate,
And this is something that I hate!

Give me chocolate every day,
Really, I'll survive that way,
But, Mum does not agree with me
And does not dish it for my tea!

Rebecca Farrugia (11)

MY NAN BISCUIT

My nan is a treasure to me,
She really means a lot.
I couldn't believe you disappeared,
You gently let me down.
I knew the time would come one day,
When you went away.
So now I live my life without you,
But I'll manage because I'm brave,
But without you my life is not the same,
And there is no one, no one to blame.
You're in my heart, you're in my soul,
Loving memories fill my head when lying in my bed.
You make laugh, you make me cry,
You make the tears come from my eyes . . .
And finally . . . you die . . .

Rebecca Elizabeth Sheppard (11)

BIRD SONG

Very early in the morning
As some are still yawning

Birds are up and singing
The air with praises ringing

They praise for an hour
Thanking God for the flower

Singing their well chosen chorus
For the ungodly and for us

Their singing was the best
So soft I laid to rest

The yawning were now awake
Toast they had to make

Chewing and eating their toasts away
Thinking of going their way

For joy the birds did bring
In joyous and happy ring.

Funmilayo Ojedokun (11)

MUM ROCKS!

Mum does the laundry -
She washes all our clothes.
She washes all the dishes
And she irons and folds.

Mum rocks! Mum rocks! Mum rocks! Yeah!

Mum takes me out each day,
She cares for me,
She gives me pocket money
And prepares my tea.

Mum rocks! Mum rocks! Mum rocks! Yeah!

Mum takes me climbing,
Tidies up,
Takes me horse riding,
Gives me drinks in a cup.

Mum rocks! Mum rocks! Mum rocks! Yeah!

Kate Bennett (8)

SHEEP AT LAMBING TIME

Lots of sheep are lambing,
Pushing and shoving,
Squelch, out comes a lamb.

Sandy Pringle (9)

WAR? WHY?

War is tragic, so many deaths,
War is a conflict between continents,
War is tragic, too much fighting,
War is in Israel, it's been going on for over thirty years.
War is tragic, all over the world,
War is World War I, II and maybe even III!
War is tragic, war is everywhere,
War is terrifying, save us before it's too late.
War needs to be prevented to save the world for the next generation,
War is tragic, what can we do to prove war is pointless
Before it happens to me or you?

Sarah George (14)

FIGHT

Two lions walk up ready to fight,
In the middle of the night.
They spot each other, let out a cry
Both look very, very sly.

Suddenly they begin to fight
Their claws scratching with all might,
They fight and fight and fight all night.

Slowly it begins to die, both let out their weak cry.
They stumble away, tripping over,
Both lay in a bunch of clover.
Their feet were covered in the mud
And body covered in their blood.

Grant Pillianz (10)

Summer Holidays

When we're at school life is boring,
We can't wait till the end of the day,
By the end of the week
We're all fast asleep
But then comes the holiday.

Six long weeks in the sun,
Hangin' with our friends,
Going to Spain
On an aeroplane,
Our luck will never end.

But by the fourth week we're missin' school
We feel it's where we belong
Seeing our school
Will be totally cool
I've not seen it for so long.

Now we're back at school, oh no,
Can't wait for the holidays to come
We all end up snoring
'Cause school is so boring
But the holidays can get dumb.

Life is so strange
When you're at school
First you don't like it
Then you think it's cool.

Rachel Forbes (11)

PIRATE POEM

A pirate was on the beach,
He was looking for me,
Suddenly he spotted some feet,
Suddenly he had a fat chest,
That ripped his vest.

Abdulroaf Ail (9)

LET'S SAVE OUR PLANET!

Let's save our planet we abuse,
Everyday it's resources we overuse,
Let's keep tidy and clean rivers,
Because the waste might end up in our school dinners!

Let's keep all our mammals alive,
Like us, give them food so they can survive!
Let's help those in needy
And learn not to be so greedy!

Let's calm down global warming, as it is a concern,
Because the disasters this year will make us learn,
That don't use up all our needed H^2O,
It is the most precious thing as you will know!

Let's not overdo our car pollution,
Because we may have difficulty finding a simple solution,
Let things in the world have a chance,
Such as trees, creatures and beautiful plants!

If we do this we don't have to pay,
For all of the things we destroyed in different ways,
So now learn not to overdo and lose
Or else there'll be nothing left so what's the use!

Do this just this once
And maybe, just maybe our world will last forever and ever!

Saima Najma (13)

IF I RULED THE WORLD

If I ruled the world no war yet no peace?
For poverty and prejudice still reign
It's up to us all to change this now for our fate and others pain
It is up to us to help save others
Strangers, friends, family, fathers and mothers.
Human greed and human war
Very unlikely to achieve more
Help me now before it's too late,
Save us from our destined fate.
If I ruled the world.

Rachael Brown (12)

IF I RULED THE WORLD

I would stop the moaning and the sighing,
Feed the homeless 'cause they're dying.
Shelter everyone when it gets wet
And make it a happy place.

I would make the police approach stronger,
'Cause when the protesters protest for longer
About our colour or our race.
If I ruled the world it would be an appealing place.

Sitting there on a humid day
Not going out to play,
The internet is not safe to have,
If I ruled the world it would be safe to use.

Trashy streets and patchy roads,
Pollution ruining fresh air and killing toads,
Oil and petrol spilling everywhere,
If I ruled the world it would not be there.

Drugs and weapons,
Bombs and war,
That goes on for ages killing more,
If I ruled the world there would be peace.

One more thing, though I have to say
My emotions have poured out today,
The rich and the poor are always needy,
Hopefully I may change the world,
Every little counts, given in little amount,
Yeah, you know about crime,
Let's bring it *down.*

Kim Matson (10)

IF I RULED THE WORLD

If I ruled the world
I would make Monday part of the weekend.

If I ruled the world
I would ban school uniform.

If I ruled the world
Nobody would have to go to work.

If I ruled the world
There would be no homework.

If I ruled the world
Everyone would be rich.

If I ruled the world
I would be queen.

Kirsty Freeman (13)

The Police

The police do their job, okay,
They're always busy every day,
Whether it's day or whether it's night
Or whether it's dark or light.

They're magnificent,
They're excellent,
They're always on the ball,
They hardly ever have a break at all.

Teri Manning (10)

IF I RULED THE WORLD

If I ruled the world,
It would be very clean.
It wouldn't have any rubbish,
On the floor to be seen.

If I ruled the world,
No trees would be cut down,
And there would be no races
Between white and brown.

If I ruled the world,
Flowers would be seen
And instead of giant towers
There would be countryside green!

Kimberley Gough (11)

IF I RULED THE WORLD

I think that if I ruled the world
I'd do a rubbish job
Let's face it, me a teenage girl
Against a World-wide mob.

The internet has taken over,
People just look on
As they become small robots
Whose brain span is now none.

Drugs own people's lives now
They take them for a laugh
A wasted life for one quick buzz
It seems a little daft!

Not to mention deadly wars
And death which stalks the streets
While people die without a cause
And others live and cheat.

Our earth has been polluted
By the gases that we've spread
For when we burn our forests
We burn our world instead.

It sounds like I'm defeated
I assure you that's not true
This world needs one to change it
Not someone who can rule.

To change the world we live in
Is something I can't do
I can only change the way I am
My question is, can you?

Jennifer Mill (13)

IF I RULED THE WORLD

If I ruled the world
I'd never stay in one place
I'd travel all over the world
And never unpack my suitcase.

I'd stop the wars in Africa
I'd give uniforms to all primary schools
I'd make sure they liked it
So I'd make it really cool.

I'd persuade more people to become policemen
And stop people polluting the air
For the animals, plants and insects
It's so unfair.

I'd ban rude websites
On the internet
Maybe even chat rooms
But definitely places you can bet!

Helen Freundlich (10)

IF I RULED THE WORLD

If I ruled the world there would be only peace
There wouldn't be any war.
If I ruled the world that fact would be stated in law.

I think in the world today
If we never had the police, danger would always be loose.
So in my world I would have robo police
So catching danger wouldn't be like chasing a wild goose.

In the world today uniform is dull and plain
If I ruled the world uniform would be colourful and insane.

The internet is great for connecting, shopping,
Getting information and communication.
If I ruled the world you would actually see who you're talking to
On the computer, face to face, it would be a great sensation.

The environment I live in today is clean and beautiful
But in other countries poor,
So In my world every country would be nice,
It would be clean, everything you saw.

Alexandra Wood (11)

IF I RULED THE WORLD

If I ruled the world!
I would always be out shopping,
My pocket money would always rise,
Hallowe'en wouldn't have apple bobbing.

Discos would last forever,
I could always watch midnight TV,
The time I went to bed would be never,
There would be no more CCTV.

The world would be made of Dairy Milk,
Trees would be made of ice cream,
Buildings would be as smooth as silk,
Grass would be a bouncy trampoline!

Victoria Newman (11)

IF I RULED THE WORLD

If I ruled the world,
This would be the law,
Let the birds fly in the sky,
Let the hunting die,
Let the fighting stop
And let the kindness spread,
There's no need to cut down trees,
Don't kill the ants and hurt the bees.
The world should be full of care!
Don't pollute the fields or the trees,
Or fill the air with smoke or fumes.
If I ruled the world,
Love and care would be the law.

Alice Gormley (9)

IF I RULED THE WORLD

If I ruled the world, no more wars or fights would be seen,
Everyone happy and peace in every land.
No more being naughty or being punished.
If I ruled the world no more killing animals
All the animals being fed night and day and being happy in winter.
Less PlayStations and more books.
If I ruled the world
More fruits and vegetables and less candy and sweets.
Also more playing with toys and less watching television.
If I ruled the world
No more board games such as Monopoly, Payday etc,
But more school studies.
Everyone would be happier if I ruled the world.

Charlotte Moore (10)

IF I RULED THE WORLD

If I ruled the world I would end all wars
Behead all serial killers,
Instead of jail criminals would be personal slaves.

If I ruled the world and school
Abolish tests of any sort,
Abolish homework, because six and a half hours of school is enough,
Just 32½ hours a week - no homework.
Teachers should be Britney Spears, Roald Dahl,
S Club 7, Blue, Beryl Kingston and A1.

If I ruled the world you would have to play by my rules.

Kerry Buckland (10)

IF I RULED THE WORLD

If I ruled the world
school would be fun!
If I ruled the world
kids would be teachers and teachers would be kids!
If I ruled the world
there'd be no more wars!
If I ruled the world
England would win the World Cup!
If I ruled the world
everyone could afford a home!
If I ruled the world
England would have the Euro!
If I ruled the world . . .
I think everyone would be happy!

Tom Dudley-Warde (11)

IF I RULED THE WORLD

If I ruled the world I'd make everything out of chocolate,
But you'd never get fat!

I'd always have loads of fun and never go to school,
You'd always have the knowledge you needed.

Everyone's wishes would always come true,
As long as they were nice!

But we have no luck as none of this is true,
It is only a poem and a very good one too!

Grace Poston-Miles (11)

IF I RULED THE WORLD

If I ruled the world I would . . .
Make more fun parks,
Let the children be safer,
Make up more sports,
Make the biggest roller coaster in the world.

If I ruled the world I would . . .
Make everyday cheaper,
Make jobs more fun and have more breaks in them,
Ban all kind of hunting,
Give the homeless homes.

If I ruled the world I'd make life fair.

Jade Preston (11)

IF I RULED THE WORLD

If I ruled the world,
There would be,
No more war,
Dividing us all.
Think of all the people,
Caught in the middle.

If I ruled the world,
There would be,
No more killing of animals,
Meant to live in the wild.
Soon, there will be no more left,
It would be all down to us.

If I ruled the world,
There would be,
No more child abuse,
Harming children,
The way they don't deserve.
Tears falling.

If I ruled the world,
There would be less pollution,
More public transport.
The future wouldn't be so grey.

None of these would happen,
If I laid down the rules.
I would be in control.
If I ruled the world . . .

Nadia Tavana (12)

IF I RULED THE WORLD . . .

If I ruled the world . . .
There would be an end to fighting,
And as I speak the world would be uniting.
If I ruled the world . . .
War would come to cease
There would be forever more, peace.
If I ruled the world . . .
Life would be worth living
The rich would help the poor, by giving.
If I ruled the world . . .
Black would also be white
People would be coloured the same
With . . . stripes.
If I ruled the world . . .
Borders and no go lines would be in the past
Everything would be happy, at last.
If I ruled the world . . .
The people that walked this earth
Would not hold hatred and discrimination,
But with love and hope
And there would be no fight, nope, nope, nope.

Leanne Bingle (12)

IF I RULED THE WORLD

If I ruled the world,
(Have no doubt),
I'd not allow war,
But keep the peace.

A criminal shall not walk,
In my world unpunished,
As they shall be helpless,
In the hands of my police.

No case shall go unsolved,
In my courts of justice,
With the best decision making judges,
And hard working, confident lawyers.

I will not allow, in my world, 'bad ISTS',
Whether it be racists or terrorists,
Not knowing how to tolerate with others,
And accept what they may believe in.

Every bad deed has a fraction of greed,
For power, money, others to have your belief,
Whatever it may be, if you're part of it,
Remember, for sure, it ends in sorrow.

So why do these bad deeds,
When you will be caught,
As there will be no point for it,
For it will not be equal to jail.

So for to settle your immense greed,
Why not receive things with good deeds?
You shall receive a bonus for those,
Which is credit for your hard work.

Ramya Salimraj (11)

IF I RULED THE WORLD

If I ruled the world
Everyone would be friends,
There would be no more guns
So we'd have to make amends.

Everyone would recycle
Have separate boxes for our bins,
One for bottles, one for plastic,
Then another one for our tins.

No one would be starving,
Or have to stand around and beg,
Everyone would be treated equal
Even if you had one leg.

There would be no more bullying
In the playground at any school
And nobody would ever again
Sit upon the dunce's stool.

All lessons would be exciting
And never again a bore,
As this would encourage children to go to school
And not to break the law.

If I ruled the world
There would be no more crime,
As I would clear up the streets
Of all the dirt and grime.

Kirsty Berry (12)

IF I RULED THE WORLD

If I ruled the world
Children wouldn't have to wear uniform to school,
Instead they could wear something cool,
Nike trainers, a baseball cap,
Maybe something from Gap.
Three quarter lengths and sleeveless tops,
Anything trendy from the shops,
If I ruled the world.

If I ruled the world
No animal would be in danger,
Animals wouldn't be scared of a single stranger,
No more killings hunting for meat,
You wouldn't even be allowed to step on their feet,
Instead they'll be happy, full of glee,
You'll go to watch them roaming free,
If I ruled the world.

If I ruled the world
Every war would stop,
No blood would be shed, not a single drop,
No gun would be fired, not a single bomb hurled,
There would be peace all over the world,
People would greet with a cheery 'Hello',
Nobody would curse, boom or bellow,
If I ruled the world.

If I ruled the world
It would be a better place,
Full of harmony and grace,
Where everyone is happy, full of glee,
Out in the world roaming free,
If I ruled the world.

Jessica Stafford (12)

IF I RULED THE WORLD . . .

If I ruled the world it would be a better place,
No discriminations against families or race.
It would all be good no matter how hard,
There would be no wars to leave you scarred.
If you all look around and take a second glance,
You will realise everyone deserves another chance.

Chelsea Pitcher (13)

IF I RULED THE WORLD . . .

What will be left?

What will be left in a hundred years time?
Will our descendants see elephants and chimps, tigers and rhino?
Will they see forests and jungles?
Will people have warm shelters, healthy lives and plenty of food?
Will they know a world of peace and a life of happiness and prosperity?
. . . Or will it be more realistic?

Where tigers and chimps are extinct,
Where instead of beautiful green forests you see ugly grey buildings,
A world where people are homeless, cold, starving and sick.
A world of war and a life of pain and suffering?
What will be left for our descendants to see?
None of us knows, but we can try and change the future for them . . .

. . . Can't we?

Maria Reali (12)

THE GRAND HUNT

Fox hunting, the cruel sport
Still no rule against it.
The race between the fox and hound.
The farmers moan about them
But if the foxes could talk, what would they say?
Could they describe their pain and fear?
Running like lightning over the countryside
Terrified animals hide!
This time! Escaping from the hunt
They're able to look after their young.

Lucas Reali (11)

IF I RULED THE WORLD

If I ruled the world
School would not exist,
Education always second,
Learning would desist.

If I ruled the world,
Greens would be outlawed,
Nothing for the children
None for the kitchen board.

If I ruled the world,
Everything for free,
Not just for everyone,
Only just for you and me.

If I ruled the world,
I'd not have a clue,
Everything on my shoulders,
What should I do!

Freyja Last (12)

IF I RULED THE WORLD

If I ruled the world
I know what I would do
I'd stop any war in its tracks
And make the enemies friends
I'd make shoplifters think twice

If I ruled the world
The environment would be cleaner
No one would litter
The flowers would flourish
No one dare pick them

If I ruled the world
Police wouldn't be needed
Everyone would behave
No hooligans or violence
Certainly no one injured intentionally

If I ruled the world in the future
Everything would change
No one would be greedy
No one would be sad
No one would be hungry
Everyone would be glad

Children can wear what they want
They can be black or white
They can be united, no racism to stop them.

If I ruled the world in the future
You'll *all* be there.

Emma Martin (12)

IF I RULED THE WORLD

Stop schools from teaching
And have a little fun,
Play football with my friends
And eat chips and beans
(But don't forget the rum).

Rapping would be at the top of the charts,
Then I would have my transport in a massive go-kart,
There would be a restaurant called Jam Tart.

Aidan Phillips (11)

IF I RULED THE WORLD

If I ruled the world I'd . . .
Call my country after my friends,
The days of the week
Would be named after my seven favourite teachers
And the months of the year
Would be named after twelve rainbow colours.

If I ruled the world I'd . . .
Make an island from jelly
So it would be really bouncy
And I'd have lots of different flavours.
The North and South Pole
Would be made from chocolate ice cream.

If I ruled the world I'd . . .
Make all houses from candy
So if you ran out of money
You could eat your house
And you could stay in bed all day
But I doubt that I will rule the world!

Hayley Sarah Johnstone (11)

WAR, NO MORE

War is bad,
War is mad,
War is insane,
War involves pain.

All wars should end,
No more need to defend,
Enough have died,
Enough have cried.

Lives have been lost,
Oh, such a heavy cost!
Uniforms no longer crease,
All rest in peace.

Beth Robertson (13)

If I Ruled The World

If I ruled the world
There would be no hate,
If I ruled the world
I'd make sure everyone had a mate,
If I ruled the world
Everyone would be kind,
If I ruled the world
Nobody would be blind,
If I ruled the world
The world wouldn't be in a mess,
If I ruled the world
Nobody would be treated any less,
If I ruled the world
Nobody would shed a tear,
If I ruled the world
Nobody would live in fear,
If I ruled the world
There would be no war,
If I ruled the world
No one would be poor.

Nicole Kay Fenwick

IF I RULED THE WORLD

If I ruled the world
I would not give you school uniform.
If I ruled the world
I would give you only two days at school.
If I ruled the world
I would make sweets free.
If I ruled the world
I would let children drive cars.
If I ruled the world
I would give you cool work to do
In school but still make sure you learn.
If I ruled the world
I would let you watch all rated films.
If I ruled the world
I would give you a free holiday
To any place you liked.
If I ruled the world
I would give everyone a million pounds
And if I ruled the world
I would actually make all of that happen.

Jessica Porter (12)

IF I RULED THE WORLD

If I ruled the world
I'd throw away war
I'd screw it up in a ball and throw it out the door.
I'd lock up all the violence
I'd lock up all the pain
I'd lock up all the hatred and never see it again.

If I ruled the world
Peace is all there would be
I'd destroy war completely, that's good enough for me
I'd destroy all the abuse
I'd destroy all the fights
I'd destroy all the pressure and throw it into the night.

If I ruled the world
I'd erase all the suffering in life
I'd let it go in the wind or stab it with a knife
I'd let go of sadness
I'd let go of war
I'd let go of everything here unless you can think of more.

Lisa Nicholls (12)

IF I RULED THE WORLD

I would ban hunting foxes
If I ruled the world,
And I'd send aid to poor countries in boxes.

Nazis and members of the Klu Klux Klan
I would ban
If I ruled the world.

Violence and war I would outlaw
If I ruled the world,
And I'd send all soldiers
Through the Job Centre door.

I'd give jobs to the unemployed
If I ruled the world.
I'd buy a time machine,
And everybody with mental health problems
I'd send back to Sigmund Freud.

Zak Hillier

PEACE

Let there be peace
Let there be light
Let there be harmony
War isn't right!

When there is peace
Every day and night
There isn't darkness
So be happy, you've got sight!

Thank you for family
Thank you for friends
Thank you for love
The world never ends . . .

Zasmeena Bancer

PEACE

Why isn't there peace on Earth?
Because we don't respect each other.
When there is war
We see darkness in the world.
Terrified people everywhere.
When there is peace
We see the light in the world.
Everyone is happy.
It's quiet
There's love and friendship.
So why war?
See if you can answer that!

Sara Wright & Emily Hirst (11)

PEACE

Peace means happiness
War means sadness
Peace means homes
War means poverty
Peace means friendship
War means hatred
Peace means health
War means dying
Peace means a dove free to roam the world
War means torment to rip the world apart
Which would you rather have?

I have friends
War could destroy them
I have family
War could destroy them
I have pets
War could destroy them
I have a life
War could destroy it
Peace if right
War is wrong.

Robert Carrington (11)

IF I RULED THE WORLD

If I ruled the world
I should be kind to others
I could make the world a better place
I might become a missionary
I would help hungry children.

If I ruled the world
I should become a vegetarian
I could stop hunting
I might stop pollution
I would help animals from dying.

If I ruled the world
I should ensure people are treated equally
I could stop white and black fighting
I might help the blacks in India, Africa and Asia
I would stop racism.

If I ruled the world
I should stop drugs
I could give money to the homeless
I might give them a home
I would help people on the streets.

Laura Hawkins (11) & Katherine Ward (10)

IF I RULED THE WORLD

If I ruled the world
I'd set the world free
And heal my family.

If I ruled the world
I'd have the power,
To bring life to every little flower.

If I ruled the world
I'd make lots of small toys
And give them to all the girls and boys.

If I ruled the world
I'd ban school uniform forever,
Even if the parents say 'Never!'

If I ruled the world
And there was a war
I'd stop them forever more.

If I ruled the world
I'd run the internet
And make it safe - no sweat!

*That's what I'd do
If I ruled the world.*

Louise Digby (10)

FREE!

If I ruled the world
There would be no taxes,
No one would be poor,
The world would be free.

If I ruled the world
No children would starve,
They could eat until they were full,
The children will be free.

If I ruled the world
There would be no criminals,
There would be no war,
The people would be free.

If I ruled the world
There would be no pollution,
There would be no hunting,
The animals would be free.

If I ruled the world
There would be no drugs,
There would be no smoking,
The doctors would be free.

If I ruled the world
There would be no terrorists,
There would be no bombing,
The world would be free.

Dominic Crawford & Simon Dunkley (11)

IF I RULED THE WORLD

If I ruled the world
I'd stop all the fighting
I'd stop all the cruelty
I'd stop all the crying
To save the world from dying!

If I ruled the world
I'd stop all the pollution
I'd stop all the dirt
I'd stop all the vandalism
To make the world a better place!

If I ruled the world
I'd stop all the suffering
I'd stop all the hunger
I'd stop all the homeless
To make the world a healthier environment!

Zasmeena Barker (11)

IF I RULED THE WORLD

If I ruled the world
I would end the poverty
And all robberies.

I could be invincible
And easily convincible.

There would be no war
And no hearts that are sore.

I am soft at heart
There will be no dark
For the people of the world.

If I ruled the world
Every girl and every boy
Will never be without a toy.

If I ruled the world
Everyone will have a safe place
In front of their eyes.

Every beggar in the streets at night
Will eventually be very bright.

If I ruled the world
It would definitely be a better place.

Thomas Filer (11) & Sebastian Timmis (10)

IF I RULED THE WORLD

If I ruled the world
I would be so strict
I could shout at all the bad people
I might become world peace maker.

If I ruled the world
I would stop animal hunting
I could make everyone vegetarians
I might save all the animals.

If I ruled the world
I would destroy all of the weapons and guns
I could stop all the wars
I might make everybody friends.

If I ruled the world
I would stop vandalism
I could undo all they had done
I might make them never do it again.

If I ruled the world
I would invent cars that run on air
I could make the air clean
I might stop pollution.

If I ruled the world
I would make all the orphans
Or homeless people have a home
I could make houses for them
And I might adopt some of them!

Sophie Smith & Naomi Wilcox (11)

IF I RULED THE WORLD

If I ruled the world
I would make it a cleaner planet
I could stop war
The world would be a safer place.

If I ruled the world
I would help the homeless
I could give to the poor
Everyone will be happy forever more.

If I ruled the world
I would lower the tax
I could make more recycling equipment
And that will help schools.

Ryan Smith & Jordan Mathias (10)

IF I RULED THE WORLD

I would stop the fighting
And make it a peaceful place,
I wish there were no homeless people
And I'd let there be happy families.

I think the lottery should be given
To people who haven't got any homes
And there be cleaner streets,
Stop smoking, no drugs.

Saving animals,
No hunting,
Make zoos cleaner,
Everyone treated equally.

Stop vandalism
All spare money to build sports centres,
Medical treatment,
Treat animals like people,
Make the world a better place.

Danielle Woodward & Katherine Stallard (10)

IF I . . .

If I ruled the world
I'd stop the war
There wouldn't be fighting anymore.

If I ruled the world
There would be happy families around
There wouldn't be bombs smashing the ground.

If I ruled the world
I would give people homes
I would give all children ice cream cones.

If I ruled the world
I'd cure the ill and helpless men
I'd make all families join again.

If I ruled the world
I'd make people see
That other people aren't what they're out to be.

If I ruled the world
I'd make all the animals become free
They wouldn't suffer like you and me.

Alex Williams & Sara Wright (11)

IF I WERE A RULER

If I were a ruler,
I'd make chocolate trees grow
We could eat all we liked
I'd make Brussels sprouts go!

If I were a ruler,
I'd make everything free
I'd help the lame walk,
I'd make the blind see!

If I were a ruler,
I'd make school like play
The teachers would agree
That we should play every day!

If I were a ruler
Machines would work well,
They'd do all our homework,
It would be swell!

Gabrielle Gleeson (9)

IF I WERE QUEEN ELIZABETH

If I were Queen Elizabeth,
All by myself alone,
I'd wear a dress of snow white silk,
And sit upon my throne.

My garden would have peacocks,
To lay golden eggs for me,
I'd have a sparkling fountain,
Beneath a willow tree.

I'd have swans with cygnets
Swimming in my pool,
I'd have lovely roses,
And it would be so cool!

Molly Schofield (8)

IF I WERE RULER

If I were Ruler,
How would I rule?
I'd make children teach adults,
I'd send them to school!
I'd show repeats of the Simpsons,
I'd teach them to ride,
I'd take them to Theme Parks
On swings and on slides.
I'd let them have sweets
And teach them to skip,
They'd play in the playground,
They'd play games of 'it'.
I'd make them get muddy
And run in the rain,
I'd make them ride bikes
And pretend to fly planes.
They could play footie
Like the girls and the boys,
I'd tear up newspapers
And replace them with toys!
They'd get pocket money
To buy children's books.
They could do colouring
And catch minnows in brooks.
Yes, If I were ruler
I'd show how it's done,
I'd get all the adults
And make them have fun!

Kate Swann (10)

IF I WERE RULER

If I were Ruler of the world
We'd travel on motorbikes
Which would have covers over them
To stop the rain getting in.
Children in schools would be given
Red and purple polos in every lesson!
And in art they'd do whatever they liked
And children could go to any class they wanted.
School uniform would be blue jeans,
With three quarter sleeved white tops
School outings would be to Africa and India
And we'd give them money if they needed it
There would be no hunting or wars
(Except brothers and sisters would be allowed to fight!)
Poor children would not have to work like slaves
And everyone would like 'The Simpsons'.

Katherine Poulter (10)

IF I WERE BOSS

If I were Boss
I'd change the schools
I'd give them more money
And I'd change the rules.

I'd make teachers
Go out to play
And in the staff room
We'd all stay!

I'd make the staff
Wear uniform
We'd all wear jeans
Every morn.

We could wear makeup
And eat sweets
And play around
It would be neat!

Elizabeth Kirk (9)

MAKING IT SAFER

If I were ruler, I'd make it safer,
I would build more hospitals
And I'd ban tobacco from the shops.
I'd be tough on drug sellers,
And I'd invent a seatbelt
That locks you in automatically.
Children would go to school
In specially designed safety minicars,
That travel at slow speed,
And stop automatically before the crash.
I'd stop any stupid wars
Because innocent people get hurt.

Jessica Mace (9)

IF I RULED THE WORLD

I am the beautiful princess,
I have golden flowing hair,
My eyes flutter like a butterfly,
But I never know what to wear!

I spend my days in Barbados,
Lying under the sun,
My servants bring me lovely food,
It is tremendous fun!

I really love to party,
I'm the coolest princess around,
I party every night
At every party I am found!

I travel in my Limo,
Or on my motorbike,
I can spend all the money
On anything I like!

I live in a palace,
It's made of shining gold!
I'd help the poor and hungry,
The helpless and the old.

I'd help all the children,
The disabled and the blind,
The deaf and the lonely,
I'd be very kind.

Sophie McDowell (9)

IF I RULED THE WORLD

I am the ruler of the world
I really like it here
Whenever I go past
People start to cheer.

My throne is made of gold
My orb has rubies red
My sceptre has got diamonds
I've a crown upon my head.

Although I am a queen
I like to water ski!
I like to play some tennis
Or go swimming in the sea.

I have chicken for my supper
And pasta for my tea
I like to help the hungry
By feeding them for free.

At Christmas I give presents
Each gets the same amount
So nobody gets jealous
The gifts I always count.

I have a cocker spaniel,
I'm very fond of her
No one would do poaching
Or kill animals for fur.

Victoria Bushnell

IF I WERE THE QUEEN OF BRITAIN

If I were the queen of Britain,
I'd like to live in Wales,
I'd have a million kittens,
Some females and some males.
I'd love to swim with dolphins,
And have pizza for my tea,
And I'd adopt a tiger,
Which would belong to me!
I'd spend my time doing art
And in English I'd write poems,
I'd go on a safari,
And then I would come home.

Harriet Morgan (8)

IF I RULED THE WORLD

Our castle would be long and wide
It'd be a mile from side to side!
We'd grow lots of money trees
You could help yourself whenever you pleased!

You could go in my Limo every day
And you wouldn't have to pay!
We'd go down to the wild blue sea
And swim with the dolphins, you and me!

We'd sit upon my golden throne
And talk to our friends on my mobile phone!
We'd see the best and coolest shows,
We'd have some really funky clothes!

We'd share my money with the poor
And they'd be happy, I am sure.
We'd always stay the bestest friends,
And this is where my poem ends.

Hannah Baker *(8)*

IF I RULED THE WORLD

If I were ruler of the world
I'd grow money trees around
I'd swim with the dolphins every day
And plant tulips in the ground!

If I were ruler of the world
My palace would be gold!
I'd have grown ups who would get me things
They'd do as they were told!

If I were ruler of the world
I'd have a Jacuzzi
I'd let some friends come in with me
But I'd be rather choosy!

If I were ruler of the world
I'd give hamsters out for free
To anyone nice who wanted one
And I'd have ninety-three!

Katie Halfhead (8)

I AM THE RULER OF THE WORLD

I am the ruler of the world,
I rule over all the land.
My king stays by my side all day,
We walk upon the sand.

I am the ruler of the world
I love the king so well,
Whenever I want a servant
I ring my silver bell.

I am the ruler of the world
My chauffeur drives my car,
It is a bright red limo
I like to go quite far!

I am the ruler of the world,
I grow a lot of flowers,
The gardener cuts the roses
In my garden I spend hours.

Alice Buys (8)

I'M A PARTYING PRINCESS!

I'm a partying princess!
I party day and night
I give my guests coconuts
And Turkish Delight!

I'm a partying princess!
I wear a gold tiara
Every day for dinner
We have spaghetti carbonara!

I'm a partying princess!
Mushrooms would be banned
So would Brussel sprouts
They're the worst in the land!

I'm a partying princess!
I'd change people's lives.
I'd give a thousand pounds
To husbands and their wives.

I'm a partying princess!
We'd all wear funky clothes
I'd help the poor and homeless
I'd give the hungry, loaves.

Georgina Williams Gray (8)

IF I RULED THE WORLD

I would have a pet husky called Spike
Who would have one white paw,
I'd live in a very tall tower made of marble
And I'd go to school only on Mondays!

I'd have a chocolate tree in my garden
And I'd have a sparkling fountain full of fish
In the middle of my flowery courtyard.

I would spend Wednesday rescuing animals
And I'd paint geraniums on Fridays,
I'd watch Sabrina, The Teenage Witch on Saturdays
And I'd play with Hannah on Tuesdays.

And I'd love to go to the moon!

I would have a necklace with exclamation marks
On it made of sapphires!

I'd have a red and white motorboat
And Dad would take me on the back of his motorbike
I'd have lots of parties and balls
And I would do anything in the world for my parents.

Amira Bushan (8)

IF I BECAME RULER OF THE WORLD

If I ruled the world
I'd live in a palace of jewels,
I'd have tigers in my garden,
And dolphins in my pools.

My peacocks would show their feathers,
My chicks would peck about,
Seahorses would bob up and down,
And water beetles dart in and out.

Laura Wheatley (9)

IF I WERE RULER OF THE WORLD

If I were ruler of the world
I'd put on shows . . .
of rolling puppies,
of growling tigers,
of leaping dolphins,
of singing blue tits.
of swinging monkeys,
of hopping rabbits,
of prowling polar bears,
of chattering parrots,
of slithering snakes.
of balancing squirrels,
of running deer,
of galloping unicorns,
of steaming dragons.
And I would invite
all the children
to come and see it
for free.

Arabella Boardman (8)

IF I WERE RULER OF THE WORLD

If I ruled the world,
I'd stop children dropping sweet wrappers,
It is such a beautiful place,
That keeping it nice, really matters.

If I ruled the world,
I'd punish those who stole,
By making them help their victims,
By delivering big bags of coal.

If I ruled the world,
I'd rule from my golden throne,
I'd give the poor some money,
So they could have a home.

If I ruled the world,
I'd invite the starving to dine,
I'd give them salad and pizza,
So they would feel fine.

Ella Shepard (8)

If I Were Ruler Of The World

If I were ruler
I would wear
Gold and silver
In my hair.

I'd have a castle,
Tall and grey,
Where the willow
Branches sway.

I'd train dogs
To bow to me,
I'd invite them
Back for tea.

I would travel
Far and wide
With a St Bernard
By my side.

Rosie Thake (9)

If I Were Ruler Of The World

If I were ruler of the world
I would ride in a silver cart
Drawn by ebony stallions,
At the crack of dawn we'd start.

I'd eat from a fine silver plate,
I'd have music in every room,
My palace would be made of gold
And I'd wear a hat with a plume.

Peacocks would strut in my courtyard,
And I'd teach magic in schools,
On Fridays we would have parties,
And after we'd swim in my pool.

Annie Moberly (8)

IF I WAS RULER OF THE WORLD

If I was ruler of the world,
I'd have five pet cats,
I'd wear long flowing dresses
And lots of fancy hats.

I'd have hedgehogs in my garden,
Penguins in my pool,
That's what it would be like,
If I were to rule.

There'd be ice cream for all my subjects,
There'd be rainbows in the sky,
We'd have sweets and cakes for dinner
And then an apple pie.

I'd grow strawberries and sunflowers,
And we'd have music all the time,
There'd be ballet and books for everyone,
And all our poems would rhyme.

I wouldn't let countries go to war,
Or argue much, or fight,
The world would be a peaceful place,
Full of joy, love and light.

Penny Hall (8)

IF I WERE RULER . . .

If I were ruler
I'd have six castles
Where my postmen
Would bring parcels.

In the parcels
Would be hats
And panda cubs
And tabby cats.

And chocolate bars
And light, blue jeans
And marshmallows
And magic beans!

Sophia Lerche-Thomsen (8)

IF I WERE QUEEN OF THE WORLD

If I were queen of the world,
No dolphins would be caught in nets,
Grown-ups would adopt wild animals,
And all children would have pets.

If I were queen of the world,
Magic would be taught in school,
We'd have lessons on babies and skating indoors
And home decorating and playing pool!

If I were queen of the world,
Everyone would run, jump and skip,
So that people would be more healthy
And everyone would be quite fit.

Camilla Hopkinson (9)

IF I WAS RULER OF THE WORLD

If I was ruler of the world
I would collect all the litter and recycle it
To make houses for the homeless.

If I was ruler of the world
I would ask everyone to help blind people
To do their shopping by reading out
What it is, and how much it costs.

If I was ruler of the world
I would ask everyone to ask a deaf person to tea
And have a conversation in sign language.

If I was ruler of the world
I would ask everyone to invite a person
Who couldn't walk, to put on a life belt
And go swimming.

If I was ruler of the world
I would ask everyone to ask a person
Who couldn't think very well
To go for a walk in the countryside
And have a picnic.

Natholia Gorvin

BIG KIDS

My mum, my mum
She shines like the sun
But she loves eating sticky buns,
She won't share them with anyone.

My dad, my dad
He thinks I'm mad,
He loves fluffy clouds
And he sucks his thumb all day.

I have three sisters
Louise loves cats,
Vicky hates bats,
Toni keeps twelve rats.

One mum,
One dad,
Three sisters,
They're all older than me
And they act like such kids.

Abbie Mackenzie (11)

MY GRAMPY LIKES . . .

My grampy's name is Dennis,
he can be a bit of a menace.
He likes his tools and building things,
he also likes to read and sing.

My grampy fixes my toys and my bike,
he likes to fish and catches pike.
He likes all of the family,
especially me!
that's why he invites me round for tea.

Because his birthday is today,
the 14th of May.
This is my present to him from me
so I hope he likes it and smiles with glee.

Jovi Slade (12)

MY BIG SISTER

My big sister loves to shop,
she comes home every day with a brand-new top.
Purple, silver, gold and blue,
I'd have thought she'd have run out of money by now wouldn't you?
Each one's different in their own style,
she always leaves them in a pile.
You'll always find her in the shops,
that's my big sister,
you really cannot miss her!

Amy Kyle (13)

MUM, MUM, YOU'RE THE BEST

She is the best, better than the rest
I give her flowers, she gives me powers
She says I'm eleven, but I'm really seven.

I gave her a fork, she gives me pork
She is the best, better than the rest
I give her a hug, I'm snug as a bug.

Clea Alakija (9)

BIG KIDS

Adults think they're ace
But we can say grace
It doesn't make them mature
We just need to learn more
That doesn't mean we're dumb
Grown-ups still suck their thumb
They really try to hide
But they're just big kids inside.

Laura Duke (13)

ADULTS, SO THEY SAY THEY ARE!

Adults think that they never make mistakes,
But when we tell them they do,
They ignore us.
Why?
I despise it when they do that,
They all think that they're right.
But one person doesn't,
I love him very much,
Who is it?
It is my number one dad.
I love him so much!
No one can take him away!

Annika Ranga

MY MAGIC MUM

If you're down and frowning
And just can't seem to smile,
She'll be there beside you and make your day worthwhile!
She loves to keep me laughing
And fun she can provide,
Just stay by her forever
And your smile will stretch for miles.
She loves to make you better,
She loves to hold you tight,
Her strong arms keep you warm, to feel loved right through the night.
With her touch you feel special,
Her magic works a treat.
She waves her wand so things aren't harmed,
She just never can be beat!

Lynsey Lee (13)

KIDS ON . . . BIG KIDS!

My Nanna is famous to everyone she knows,
Not for her singing or dancing,
Or even because she sews.
Not for photography or painting,
Or because she is good looking,
She is famous for her wonderful cooking.
Bread, pies, scones and cakes,
All of these she can make,
But best of all, the best there can be,
She makes omelettes every Wednesday for Becky and me!

Hannah Watson (13)

A STRANGE SPECIES!

The adult is a strange species,
It's an early riser
And a cleaning fanatic
And its favourite game is 'Nag the Kids'.
I mean, how strange can you get
And what happened to fashion?
It's amazing what you find around the world nowadays!

Vicki Bennett (14)

A Housewife's Job

A housewife's job is not so easy
Because you know you're stuck being busy,
There's washing, ironing and dusting too,
Don't forget you've got to clean the loo!
Quick, make dinner, cook tea as well,
Pick up kids after the school bell.
Your husband comes in with his shoes a mess
Grab the shoe wax and brush; your jobs don't get less.
After tea (which has quickly been eaten)
You start to feel like you've been beaten,
Of course you know it is not a sin
Just to clear out that horrid bin.
You come back from shopping, that means you've been buying
Time to sit down but the baby starts crying,
His nappy needs changing as well as a feed
Every day feels like you're always in need.
The day seems to come to an end,
Your mind feels like it's been round the bend.
A housewife's job isn't a piece of cake,
The next morning you'll have to wake.

Emma Davenport (11)

PARENTS

Parents, huh don't you just hate them.
I can guarantee that when visitors come round for tea
the dreaded photos come out of me.

There's one of me in the bath completely naked
playing with my dollies.
I got revenge when I brought out the pictures
of my mum on the beach in her bikini
and when Dad dived into the pool
(thinking he was really good)
and his trunks fell down
showing his very large bottom to everyone!

There is one other thing I hate about my parents.
Whenever I start eating chocolate, my mum shouts
and says, 'Stop eating that chocolate, it will rot your teeth.'
So she sends me up to my room,
but when I come back down I see empty wrappers everywhere.

I wish I could magic up my own cool parents
and not my own boring, embarrassing parents!

Annabel Gray (11)

MY NAN, MY MATE

My nan is just so great
She's not just 'Nanny', but my mate
I love her smell, her mouth, her eyes
She's like a scented flower in disguise

She's just so beautiful, it's hard to bear
She's generous, loving, hugging and fair
I love my nan so, so much
She's got the most gentlest touch

I get excited whenever I see her
Sometimes I just wish I could be her
She buys the bestest ever toys
Whatever I like, she enjoys

She's better than all the other nans
She's far too young to be called 'Gran'
So if you think your nan's the best
Think again because mine's better than the rest!

Natalie Whiffin (13)

KIDS ON BIG KIDS

Why is our world like what it's like? Why don't our parents
take a hike?
They always tell us what to do! I hate the way they shout at you!
And the way they always treat us bad, and take the good things that
we've had!
They always stop you having fun, and tell you off for things
you've done!
They always moan at you and say 'Tidy that room, right now! Today!
Don't answer back, don't give me cheek or else you're grounded
for a week!'
Other adults are just as bad, they all forget the fun they've had,
When they were little children too, but they still all go and pick on you!
'Oh just grow up! Do this, do that! Stop being a spoiled little brat.'
It never ends, they just go on, they don't care, not a single one.
They shout and nag and sceam and cry, they smack and moan,
but why or why!
They ruin your life and then they say 'You'll thank me for this,
you know, one day.
I'm doing this for your own good! If only you behaved the way
you should!'
They moan and moan at us all day! And teachers, well, they all say
'Don't do that! Stop wasting time! Stop telling lies and do not mime
Or mimic me in any way! That's a detention for today!
Don't make excuses, that isn't true. How many times have I told you.'
They're just as bad, they're all the same, and they say the parents
are to blame!
And old people all live in the past, they try to make us grow up too fast!
And throw our childhood all away and they've always got too
much to say!
They shouldn't be the way they are, they always moan and go too far.
They're strict to us and always lie! Get on your nerves and always sigh.
Adults always boss us kids around and from their mouths comes an
awful sound!
The sound of someone always nagging! Someone who desperately
needs gagging!

Adults are hypocrites and don't lead by example at all, it's one rule
for them, another for us, or so I recall,
They act as if we're the bad guys, well they're in for a big surprise!
Because one look in the mirror will make them see, they're just a larger
image of you and me!

Lisa Booth (14)

KIDS ON BIG KIDS

If I were an adult,
I could boss people around,
and get what I want.
If I were an adult,
I'd b a partner to someone,
and a parent to others.
I'd have to make quick decisions,
and be responsible for them too.
I'd get the blame,
If something went wrong,
and I'd have to work
loads of hours.
No, I think I'll just stick
to being a kid.

Hannah Coope

MY HEAD TEACHER

My head teacher is the best,
If you like hearing . . .
'Tuck in your shirt. Tie up your laces.
How long is your skirt?
All you children, can't you see?
That no one is bigger and better than me!'

But I think that when he's alone,
He plays with his plastic animal toys,
And has pretend fights with his soldier boys.
When he walks home, he passes the pub,
He plays on the swings and falls in the mud.

So, when he's at school, he's a loud, mean creature,
But when he's at home, he's a secret teacher.

Hattie Ball (11)

PARENTS

Huh! Parents! Don't you just hate them?
I can almost guarantee that whenever the nice neighbours
Come round for a grown-up talk, the dreaded videos of me, come out.
There's one of me on the potty, saying my first word.
Guess what it was?
Poo!
But I have my tactics to get revenge.
I get the photos out of when we were on our family holiday.
There's one of my dad running around the pool,
trying to look cool, then he slips, falls on his nose and
slides head first into the pool, taking his trunks off in the process.
How embarrassing!
There's this other photo which really gets on my mum's nerves,
when dad secretly took a photo of my mum when she had just got up!
That will teach her to put a face-mask on in bed!

Jessica Parsons (10)

BIG KIDS ON LITTLE KIDS!

Normally teachers are . . .
Boring
Bossy
Brainy, and think they know it all
Sad and strict
Chatty and blab on
Nag too much
Wicked mean people!

But my teacher is . . .

Funky!
I mean who else wears bright pink Doc Martin's shoes?
And she's still running round, playing hockey,
Now when she's even a grandma!
Sometimes she's out of her mind.
So kind and helpful, fair as well!

That's why I like my teacher the best!

Kayleigh Jayne Powell (10)

NEXT-DOOR NEIGHBOURS
(For Alison Bailey)

Next-door neighbours
Come in all shapes and sizes
But no one's quite like mine.

She has short brown hair and blue eyes
Looks a lot younger than she really is.
Whenever I go there, she always seems quite bouncy.
She never moans and she's reasonably funny.
She loves her kids (oh, yes I forgot!)
Really, I don't know how she manages her oldest (Amelia).
Her youngest (Annabelle), she's cute!
Although I love them both.

Next-door neighbours
Come in all shapes and sizes.
But mine, never changes!

Ali Newsom

MY NEXT-DOOR NEIGHBOUR

My next-door neighbour
Is going into labour,
Although she has five boys
Who make lots of noise.
They play Sum 41
Which I think is dumb.

She hopes for a girl
To call her Pearl,
All the others were boys,
Who break all their toys.
And that is my next-door neighbour.

Phoebe Welham & Eloise Wood

KIDS ON BIG KIDS

I'm looking for my big tough dad,
he's playing with a shopping bag.

There's my cheerful mum
eating a large fat bun.

My brother's here, he's with his friend
they're driving me round the bend.

And that is all of them you see,
the ones I call my family!

Louise Cockle (10)

KIDS ON BIG KIDS

I think my mum is the best, although when she wants to, she nags,
She's really good because she's kind and never lets us wear rags.
My dad could win a prize for being the most rudest and annoying.
Then there's his awful habit of burping at weekends, and his
noisy yawning.
Jane, my next door neighbour, is friendly enough and caring,
But thanks to dad, I don't want to know if she can sing!
On the other side lives Clair, who has the most wonderful hair,
Her sons, Harry and George drive her crazy, I'm sure it doesn't
seem fair!

Mrs Edmonds is a favourite teacher, of course
She used to be teased about having a neck like a horse!
Mrs Price is another favourite teacher of mine,
I have known her since I started school, which is a long time!
Mrs James is another favourite, she's my actual teacher,
I think she's very nice.
She's taught me before, quite a while ago-
Three years ago, to be precise!
All the teachers at Carswell can be very strict,
But all of them are very nice, you'll find this out quick!

These are the best of the grown-ups around me I know,
But they all have one thing in common,
They don't like the snow!

Alice Samways (9)

ANIMAL ALPHABET

You go to a zoo
To look at the animals,
But they're all looking at you.

A ntelopes, look funny at you
B aboons and bullocks, look scary at you
C ats and cobras hiss at you
D ogs and dingoes run up to you
E lephants stamp at you
F ish splash water at you
G orillas jump all over the place
H ippopotami try to eat you
I nsects fly at you
J aguars try to scare you
K oala bears love you
L ions roar at you!

Jake Tonge, William Garratt & Kyle Phillips (7)

MY DAD

He is crazy
He is cute
He likes footballs being beaut
He is lovely
Great hair
He is really quite fair
He likes beer
But I love him because
He is nearly always here.

Jessica Port (12)

OUR TROUBLED WORLD

This planet is a funny world
I believe I'm lucky to be in it
Although many wars never seem to stop
Nobody cares one bit.

People always arguing, police trying to solve,
Animals get killed, landscape fading.

Everyone wishes this world a happy place to be
As the news headlines scream every day.

However, people should not fear this,
Schools are talking about it too,
The future depends on us now
We people, have got a lot of things to do.

Adnan Haq (12)

KIDS ON BIG KIDS

Today at home, I hurt my knee
My mum took good care of me.
My knee is sore
It bleeds more and more,
She washes the blood away
She's special in May.
She sticks a plaster on me
It hurts me.
That's my mum!

Lauren Shaw (10)

KIDS ON BIG KIDS

My mum is a pain
but she cares for me,
My dad is cool
but he works too hard.
Teachers are the worst of all,
Especially our teacher bringing in sewage water.

Sarah-Louise Gee (10)

KIDS ON BIG KIDS

This morning I hurt my knee
Mrs Atkin looked after me,
She bandaged it up
And got me some water, in a cup.
Mrs Tucker got me an ice-pack,
Then Mrs Nobbs got me a small sack.
I went back to class
We had a small task,
Then it was break time
And then I was fine!

Faron Lilly (10)

KIDS ON BIG KIDS

My mum, my mum
My very special mum.
She's got a tiny tum
and she really hates rum.
She's got brown eyes
and she really loves pork pies.
She loves her shopping,
but she doesn't do much hopping.
My mum, my mum
I really love my mum.

Faye Humphrey (10)

KIDS ON BIG KIDS

My grandad is a big kid
He wishes he ruled the world,
I bet he'd have a tickling machine,
To tickle me on my belly.
And lots of sweets for him and me.
He doesn't know I think this of him, but . . .
He gets in a huff when he doesn't win,
He makes a terrible din.
He shouts at me when I take his sweets
But he isn't any better.

Charlotte Garforth (10)

KIDS ON BIG KIDS

Adults are ridiculous
Teachers are the worst,
Kids are fantastic
Alexandra's first.
The biggest kid in the whole wide world
Is definitely my teacher.
She brings in dirty sewage water
Which is a nasty feature.
She laughs a lot
And plays all day.
Okay, she's nice
In some kind of way.

Katharine Chatters (10)

KIDS ON BIG KIDS

Teachers are quite a pest
Don't you agree, kids need a rest?

Kids definitely have to rule,
All big kids do is sit and drool.

Mums and dads are just as bad
They do complain quite a tad.

You have to do something about this,
All we need is a little bliss!

Sally Kaldas (10)

KIDS ON BIG KIDS

My best nurse definitely is not a curse,
My best cycle teacher, could hop a metre,
My best SATs helper, helps me a lot
My best cook, you've gotta take a look
My best man, would never hurt me
Or desert me!
My best mum would never leave me,
Never, ever, ever!

Lorna Griffiths (10)

KIDS ON BIG KIDS

She is funny
Her nose is always runny,
She looks after me
And gives me my tea,
She is my mum
She has a small bum.
Her belly is made of jelly,
She is never nasty.
She's always nice,
But the thing she really hates are mice!

Casey Wright (10)

KIDS ON BIG KIDS

My grandad is mad,
He is really bad.
He does everything with me,
He's always hurting his knee.
My grandad likes football
He doesn't like the Mall.
My grandad's cool!

Laurence Taylor (10)

KIDS ON BIG KIDS

The big kid here is
My teacher, she brings in
Icky water and other stuff.
She acts like a little girl,
And has a big pearl.

Sam Coe (10)

My Mum, The Shopping And TV Fanatic

My mum, my mum,
She really is obsessed
She loves to watch the news and soaps
She likes the chat shows best.

My mum, my mum,
She also loves to shop.
Whenever we are going out,
She'll buy and never stop!

My mum, my mum,
It's shops, that she adores.
She races through the clothes shops
And searches outlet stores!

My mum, my mum.
She's TV and shopping mad,
But after taking a little thought
She really ain't all that bad.

My mum, my mum
She has her ups and downs,
But my real thoughts on my mum are
That she's great, all round!

Marc Dragon

MY GROOVY OLD GRAN

My groovy old gran,
Is one of a kind,
She's well past eighty
And out of her mind.

She's been everywhere,
And done everything,
She loves a good dance
And loves a good sing.

She's been to Kenya,
China and Chile,
She brought back a snake,
I think she's plain silly.

She's been scuba diving,
Kayaking as well,
She also goes skiing,
And does them all well.

She loves down the disco,
Every Saturday night.
With all her great moves
She's an eye-popping sight.

Although she is crazy
And acts like the fool.
At the end of the day,
I still think she's cool.

Gemma Gibbs (10)

KIDS ON BIG KIDS

Miss Frith!

She's fantastic,
She's cool,
She's funny,
She's hip,
She's my drama teacher.
Her name's Miss Frith,
She always makes her lessons fun,
When I get home, I always tell my mum,
After a stressful day at school.
It's drama time,
Which always rules,
We perform our plays on the stage,
She gives us scripts, page after page.
She takes us all at an equal pace,
She's always got a smile on her face!

Abigail Bradford (11)

KIDS ON BIG KIDS

At school I used to have a teacher,
She was my favourite, and I miss her,
My mum is nice, my dad is kind
They never ever leave me behind.
My next door neighbour has a bunny,
He makes me laugh, he's very funny.
All in all, adults are fun,
I can't wait, 'til I am one.

Stacey Sims (11)

ADULTS

They shout and they moan,
they'll tell you to
'Leave me alone!'
They're just big kids.

Some of them smell,
they don't wash very well.
They sing when they win.
They're just big kids.

They play with our games
and call us names.
They boo you when
they lose to you.
They're just big kids.

Some drive you crazy
others are plain lazy,
They even act like babies
cos they're just big kids.

They're loaded with money
but say they don't have any.
They spend it all on alcohol
so they won't look like kids.

When they're not sad
they make you feel glad,
They'll play with you in the park
and have a good laugh.
After all, they're just big kids!

Nisha Haq (9)

FLOWERS

Flowers are wonderful, growing all around,
Flowers start off as a seed, planted in the ground.
Flowers are colourful,
Never dull.
Flowers are just so beautiful.

I think all flowers should stand up tall,
So everybody can enjoy looking at them all.
I love to see flowers in the spring,
To look at them is a lovely thing.

Thanks for reading my poem today,
I hope you have had a lovely day.

Samantha Dolley (11)